The Weather Today

Written by Jenny Feely
Series Consultant: Linda Hoyt

WorldWise™
Content-based Learning

Contents

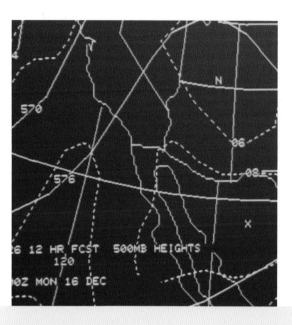

Chapter 1

What's the weather like today?

What will the weather bring today? A perfect sunny day with blue sky stretching as far as you can see? Stormy skies with lightning flashing? Gale-force winds that can push strong trees over? **Humid** weather where the air seems to ooze or drip with water? The weather can bring all of these things and more.

Weather is the name given to all the sorts of conditions of the air that we find when we go outdoors. Most of the time weather is mild and not dangerous. Sometimes weather can be extreme and very dangerous. Then people need to know what they should do to keep themselves safe.

Where does weather come from?

The earth is surrounded by a layer of air called the **atmosphere**. This is where all weather happens. As the wind, temperature, cloudiness and moisture in different parts of the atmosphere change, so does the weather.

All changes in the weather happen because of the effects of the sun's heat on the earth. During the day, the sun warms the air, the land and the water. During the night, without the sun's heat, the air, the land and the water cool. This creates wind, rain and differing temperatures.

When air is heated, it moves upwards, and when water is heated, it evaporates into the air. The moving air and evaporated water mix in the atmosphere to make weather.

Layers of the atmosphere

The atmosphere starts at the earth's surface and extends towards space for about 560 kilometres.

| Exosphere |
| kilometres |
| 500 |

400

Orbiting satellite

300

Thermosphere

200

100

Meteor

80

Mesosphere

45

Stratosphere

Weather

Aeroplane

10

Troposphere

Highest mountains

7

Chapter 2

Wind and rain

Where does wind come from?

Wind is moving air because air moves up when it is warmed by the sun. The warmed air pushes cooler air out of the way and makes it move too. The air in the **atmosphere** is warming and cooling all the time so there is a lot of windy weather.

Where breezes come from

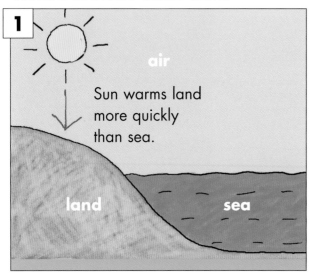

1 Sun warms land more quickly than sea.

air

land   sea

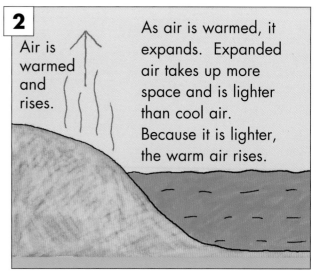

2 Air is warmed and rises.

As air is warmed, it expands. Expanded air takes up more space and is lighter than cool air. Because it is lighter, the warm air rises.

3 Cooler air moves inland to fill the space left by the warmer air. This air movement is wind.

cool air

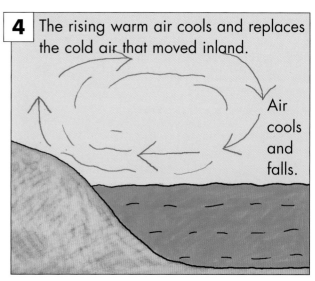

4 The rising warm air cools and replaces the cold air that moved inland.

Air cools and falls.

Warm some air

You will need:

A balloon
Sticky tape
Two large bowls
Hot water and cold water

What to do

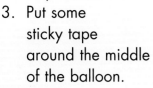

1. Fill one bowl with hot water and the other with cold water.
2. Blow up the balloon so that it is about 3/4 of its possible size.

3. Put some sticky tape around the middle of the balloon.
4. Put the balloon in the hot water. What happens?
5. Put the balloon in the cold water. What happens?

Why it happens

The hot water heats the air in the balloon, making it expand. As it expands, the air takes up more space, which makes the balloon get bigger. When you place the balloon in the cold water, the air in the balloon gets colder. This makes it take up less space, or contract.

Make some wind

You will need:

A very thin piece of paper
A lamp
A piece of cotton thread
Scissors

What to do

1. Draw a spiral on the paper and cut it out.
2. Tie the thread onto the middle of the spiral.
3. Turn the lamp on.
4. Hold the spiral over the lamp. What happens?

Why it happens

The light bulb heats the air around it. As the air gets warmer, it rises. As the air moves, it pushes the spiral. This is what happens when air is warmed by the sun. The moving air is called wind.

Where does rain come from?

There is a lot of water in the atmosphere. When it is heated by the sun, the water changes into a gas called water vapour. This process is called **evaporation**. The water vapour rises up into the atmosphere, and as it rises the water vapour cools and tiny droplets form. You can see these droplets as they make up clouds.

When the tiny droplets collide with dust in the air, bigger droplets form. These droplets fall as rain when the droplets get too big to stay in the air. This is called **precipitation**.

The rain cycle

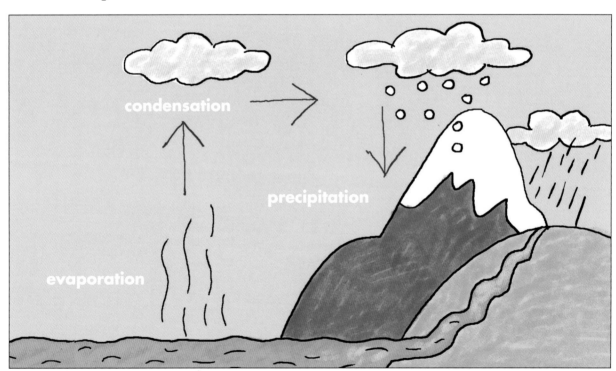

Evaporation
The sun's heat turns water from a liquid to a gas.

Condensation
Water vapour cools and becomes tiny droplets.

Precipitation
Water droplets fall to the earth as rain. If it is very cold, droplets freeze, forming ice, snow, sleet or hail.

Did you know?

Scientists believe that there is about the same amount of water on Earth now as there was when the dinosaurs roamed the planet.

Make some rain

You will need:
A glass bowl
A china plate
Hot water
Ice cubes

What to do

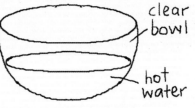

clear bowl

hot water

1. Pour 5 centimetres of very hot tap water into a glass bowl.

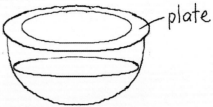

plate

2. Cover the bowl with a plate.

ice cubes

3. Place some ice cubes on the plate. What happens?

Why it happens

When the warm air in the bowl touches the cold plate, the moisture in the air condenses and forms water droplets (rain). This is what happens in the atmosphere as warm, moist air rises and is cooled.

Chapter 3

What's happening outside?

What's the weather like today?

On any one day there is all sorts of weather around the world. Look at the map to see temperatures and weather for one day in February. February is late winter in the northern hemisphere and late summer in the southern hemisphere.

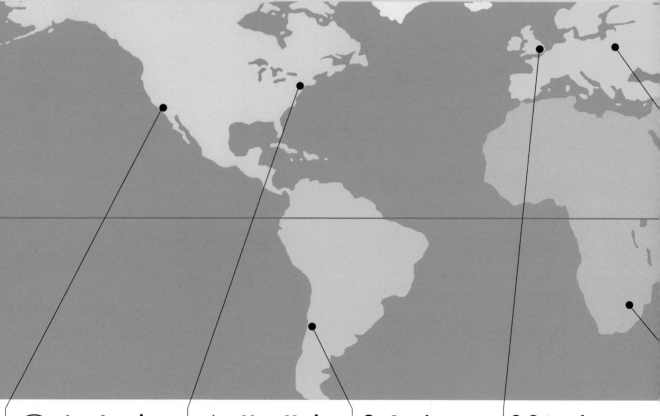

Los Angeles
17°C
In Los Angeles it is humid. The sun is shining, but the air is wet.

 New York
3°C
In New York there is sleet. It is cold and wet.

● **Santiago**
30°C
There are showers in Santiago. It is very warm.

●● **London**
6°C
In London it is cold and rainy. Earlier there was frost.

International weather symbols

◯	clear sky	●	some rain	thunderstorms	=	mist
◑	cloudy sky	●●	heavy rain	hurricane	≡	fog
◕	very cloudy sky	✳	some snow	sandstorm or dust storm	❟	intermittent drizzle
●	overcast sky	✳ ✳	heavy snow	sleet	❟❟	steady drizzle

Northern hemisphere

Equator

Southern hemisphere

Johannesburg
29°C
In Johannesburg it is overcast. Sometimes there is light drizzle.

✳✳ **Moscow**
−11°C
In Moscow it is snowing. It is very cold.

Singapore
34°C
In Singapore it is stormy. Lightning lights the sky.

Melbourne
36°C
Melbourne is hot and dusty. Hot air is blowing from the desert.

13

Extreme weather

Although weather can be inconvenient or annoying at times, most weather is not dangerous. But sometimes the weather is much more extreme and can hurt or kill people. During wild weather, people must be very careful to make sure they are as safe as possible.

Blizzards are intense winter storms with winds of 55 kilometres per hour or higher. Blizzards have falling or blowing snow, which reduces visibility below 400 metres for three hours or more.

During lightning storms, enormous and very hot sparks of electricity develop in the clouds. The electricity moves from the clouds to the earth as lightning. As a lightning bolt travels to the ground it can heat the air to 30,000°C Celsius. This sudden change of air temperature creates the crash of thunder that follows the lightning.

During hailstorms, frozen drops of water fall to the ground. Some hailstones are as big as soccer balls. Hail can dent cars, break windows, strip the leaves off trees and destroy crops.

Tornadoes are funnel clouds in spinning columns of air. Tornadoes drop out of severe thunderstorms. They can be 600 metres wide and travel at speeds of 70 kilometres per hour. They usually last only a few minutes but can lift houses into the air and rip trees from the ground. Tornadoes that occur over water create waterspouts.

Hurricanes are intense storms with swirling winds up to 240 kilometres per hour. Hurricanes are 1,000 to 5,000 times larger than tornadoes. They are usually around 480 kilometres across. Hurricanes are also known as cyclones and typhoons.

If winds of 65 kilometres per hour or greater are expected to occur for at least one hour, a high wind warning will be issued. Some winds cause sandstorms.

15

How can we predict the weather?

Looking at clouds can be one of the easiest ways to predict the weather. Clouds have different shapes, depending on the weather conditions when they form. They can tell us a lot about what to expect from the weather.

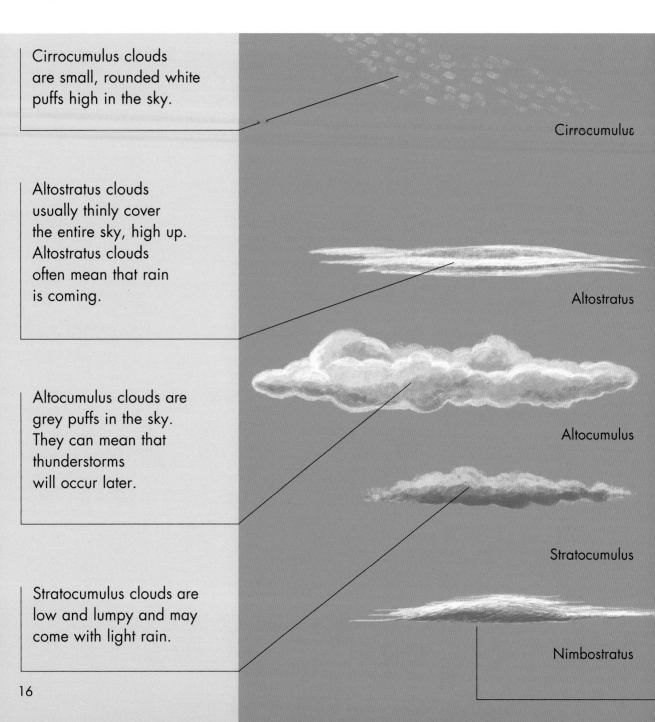

Cirrocumulus clouds are small, rounded white puffs high in the sky.

Cirrocumulus

Altostratus clouds usually thinly cover the entire sky, high up. Altostratus clouds often mean that rain is coming.

Altostratus

Altocumulus clouds are grey puffs in the sky. They can mean that thunderstorms will occur later.

Altocumulus

Stratocumulus

Stratocumulus clouds are low and lumpy and may come with light rain.

Nimbostratus

Have you ever been out in the fog?
Then you have walked inside a cloud.
Fog is a cloud that touches the ground.
Fog forms on nights that are clear and
damp. Warm, wet air near the ground
cools and moisture in the air condenses.
This forms a very low cloud.

Cirrus

Cumulonimbus

Cumulus

Stratus

Cirrus clouds are clouds
that form up high. They
are thin and icy.

If cumulus clouds get
very tall and high, they
can bring heavy rain
or thunderstorms.
Then they are called
cumulonimbus clouds.

Cumulus clouds sit low in
the sky. They look fluffy.
They usually occur when
the day is fine.

Stratus clouds are thin, low
and wide. They can get
big enough to cover the
sky. When stratus clouds
get thick, they cause rain or
snow. Then they are called
nimbostratus clouds.

Chapter 4

Forecasting the weather

Interview with a meteorologist

Meet Eva. She's a meteorologist. She studies the weather and makes weather forecasts.

Q. What do you do?

A. I work as part of a team of meteorologists. We collect and look at data about the weather. We measure many things including temperature, rainfall, wind speed and direction, and the pressure of the **atmosphere**.

Q. How do you get this information?

A. Weather information comes from all over the world and from space. Satellites, aeroplanes, ships, weather balloons and weather stations collect weather information.

Q. What do satellites do?

A. Satellites **orbit** the earth, collecting information about the weather below them. They can take pictures of clouds, showing if they are high or low. They can take pictures that show what parts of the earth are warm or cool. They can also test how wet the atmosphere is and how clean the air is.

Q How do meteorologists use the information?

A. After putting together all the information we have collected, we analyse it. We then report about what the weather has been like over a time period, say the last 24 hours, and predict what the weather is likely to be like for the next few days. We also use the information collected to see how it fits into long-term weather patterns. This helps us to predict things like droughts.

Q. Weather forecasts are sometimes wrong. Why is that?

A. Sometimes weather predictions are wrong because a very small change in conditions can cause very large changes in the weather. These changes are too small to measure, but have a huge impact on the way the weather turns out. As our ways of collecting and analysing weather information get better, our weather forecasts are becoming more reliable and accurate.

Q. Do you like being a meteorologist?

A. Yes, I do. **Meteorology** is an extremely important science. Extreme weather is dangerous and by telling people to be careful we can save their lives. Even knowing that we have helped people lead more comfortable lives by giving them good weather information is very satisfying.

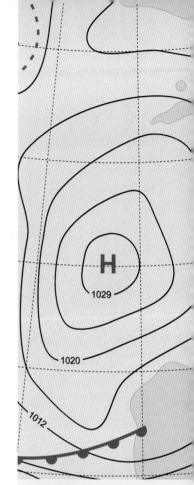

Did you know?

Look up weather data for your town for the last month. Can you find any patterns in the data? What does the information tell you about what the weather might be like tomorrow? Make a weather forecast for the next three days. At the end of the three days check to see if your forecast was accurate.

Technology for predicting the weather

Effective weather prediction depends on collecting a lot of accurate information about wind, rainfall, air pressure and humidity from many different places. To do this, many different instruments, machines and computers have been developed and are used in weather stations.

At some weather stations, there are people living nearby to collect the weather data. Other weather stations are in isolated places. The data from isolated places is collected and sent to meteorologists so that they can predict the weather.

A weather station in the mountains

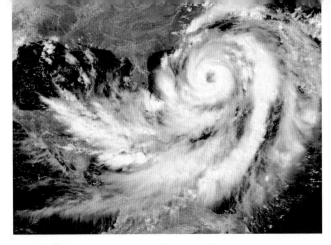

Satellite picture of hurricane

Weather satellites take pictures of weather from high above the surface of the earth. The pictures show huge amounts of weather conditions at one time. Meteorologists use these pictures to see weather patterns and predict events such as hurricanes.

Weather balloon

Meteorologists use weather balloons to collect data from the atmosphere. Weather balloons are filled with helium, which is lighter than air, so they can float high into the air. They carry devices that measure temperature, humidity and air pressure.

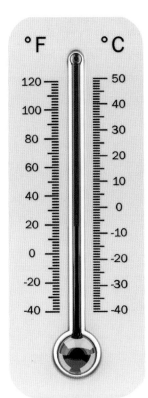

A thermometer measures air temperature.

A barometer measures air pressure.

A hygrometer measures how much water vapour is in the air. The more water vapour in the air, the more likely clouds will form and rain will fall.

Build your own weather station

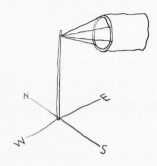

You can collect data about the weather near you. You can work out weather patterns and try to predict what the weather will be like tomorrow.

A weather station needs:

A wind sock
A rain gauge
A thermometer
A chart for your observations

Make a rain gauge
You will need:

An empty plastic bottle
Scissors

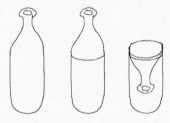

1. Cut the top off the bottle.
2. Put the top inside the bottom so that it fits snugly.
3. Put the bottle outside in a shallow hole.
4. Check how much rain has collected in your rain gauge at the same time each day.

Make a wind sock
You will need:

A plastic bag
A pipe cleaner
Sticky tape
String
Scissors

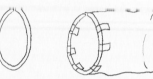

1. Make a circle with the pipe cleaner.
2. Cut a hole in the end of the plastic bag.
3. Tape the opening of the bag over the pipe cleaner circle.
4. Tie the string to the pipe cleaner in four places.
5. Hang your wind sock outside.
6. Mark north, south, east and west on the ground near your wind sock.
7. Check the wind direction each day.

Make a weather record chart for your observations

1. Collect data for each day. Use this information to report the weather for that day.
2. Use the data to predict what the weather will be tomorrow.
3. The next day, check to see how accurate your predictions were.

Glossary

atmosphere the air surrounding the earth

condensation when water vapour changes from a gas into a liquid

drizzle light rain made up of small water droplets

evaporation when the sun's heat turns water from a liquid into a gas

fog a cloud near or on the ground

frost white ice crystals that form on flat surfaces, created when water vapour in the air freezes

humid when there is a lot of evaporated water in the air

meteorologist a scientist who studies weather and makes weather predictions

meteorology the science of weather and weather forecasting

orbit to circle around

overcast when a widespread layer of clouds covers all of the sky

precipitation when water falls to the earth as rain

shower a short period of rain

sleet small ice pellets, formed when raindrops freeze near the surface of the earth

Index